Getting the Most From Your
AROMA® RICE COOKER

Coleen and Bob Simmons

BRISTOL PUBLISHING ENTERPRISES
Hayward, California

CONTENTS

2 A Cooker for the World's Most Versatile Food

3 About Rice Cookers

3 Rice Cooker Accessories

8 Basic Ingredients for the Rice Cooker

11 Recipes: Basic Rice and Side Dishes, Salads, Soups, Main Dishes, Seafood, Poultry, Vegetables, Other Dishes and Desserts

---

A **nitty gritty**® cookbook

©2005 Bristol Publishing Enterprises,
2714 McCone Ave., Hayward, CA 94545.
1-800-346-4889

Printed in China.
ISBN 1-55867-324-5

Cover design: Frank J. Paredes
Cover photography: John A. Benson

FOR A FREE CATALOG OF ALL OUR BOOKS, CALL BRISTOL PUBLISHING TOLL-FREE AT 1-800-346-4889

Congratulations on your purchase of an **AROMA** rice cooker. As makers of the number-one brand of rice cookers in America, we're pleased to see the rice cooker becoming a staple appliance in American kitchens. Our goal has always been to make this incredibly useful and versatile appliance as essential to the American lifestyle as a toaster or coffee maker.

For this cooker, we wanted to bring our customers something very special. We want to make sure you can get the most from your rice cooker —and that includes many uses you may not have thought of. For example, who would have thought you could make a tasty lemon custard in a rice cooker? That's what makes this cookbook special. The authors, Coleen and Bob Simmons, have done a wonderful job creating deliciously tempting recipes that make full use of the versatility of rice cookers.

From rice blends to salads to whole meals, we think you'll be amazed and thrilled as you discover all of the wonderful dishes you'll be able to make with your new rice cooker. Enjoy.

—The **AROMA** Family

A COOKER FOR THE WORLD'S MOST VERSATILE FOOD

One half of the world's population eats rice at least once a day. For these people a rice cooker is the most sought-after kitchen appliance. Not only does it cook rice perfectly every time, but it will keep rice warm and delicious for several hours after cooking.

Because the cooker is always used for rice, usually cooked plain, other uses are rarely explored. The rice cooker makes a perfect vegetable steamer, and can be used to prepare a variety of delicious, healthful one-dish meals that can be served directly from the cooker. In addition we include several recipes that start with cooked rice for a base and some old favorite recipes that are served over cooked rice. Dim sum, the delightful Chinese snacks, can be easily made ahead and steamed in the rice cooker just before serving.

The rice cooker is a handy appliance for the home kitchen, the dorm room or studio apartment, the kitchen remodel or the ski cabin. It is an all-purpose pot. Consider using it to cook frozen vegetables or entrées in pouches, or to steam fresh vegetables, fish or chicken. It also can be used as a stew or soup pot, or for making risotto. It is much faster to reheat foods in the rice cooker by steaming rather than using an oven.

ABOUT RICE COOKERS

All **AROMA** Rice Cookers will produce perfectly cooked rice if properly used.

All "on-off" or "cook-hold" rice cookers work on the same principle. An inner pan sits on a heated plate that brings water in the pan to a boil. The water boils vigorously until it is absorbed by the food, or boils off as steam. A temperature sensor in contact with the pan senses the rise in temperature above that of boiling water and reduces the heat to "warm," which keeps the contents of the pan at the proper serving temperature without burning.

RICE COOKER ACCESSORIES

The rice cooker comes with a steamer tray, a rice measuring cup, a soup ladle and a flat rice serving spoon. There are several other accessories that will make rice cooker recipes even easier. You may already have some of these items in your kitchen.

A long-handled plastic spoon is very handy to have when using the rice cooker. Long-handled to keep your hands away from the steam and hot sides of the cooker when stirring or dishing up, and plastic so as not to scratch the nonstick finish in the bottom of the pan. This spoon is also handy for scraping rice grains from the bottom of the pan during cleanup.

Depending on the size of your cooker pan, you may find a bamboo steamer basket that will fit down about halfway into the cooker pan. The 8-inch size is perfect to use in a cooker that is about 9 inches across the top.

Bamboo steamer baskets can be stacked two or three high to steam individual plates of fish or chicken, and also make it possible to do larger quantities of dim sum or timbales. Use the bamboo lid on the top steamer. If necessary, wedge a clean dishtowel between the steamer basket and the rice cooker pan to prevent excessive loss of steam.

HELPFUL HINTS

If your rice cooker pan is not coated with a nonstick surface, be sure to spray the rice cooker pan liberally with a high quality nonstick cooking spray. This will make cleanup much easier. The spray adds very little either in flavor or calories.

We use kosher salt in the rice cooker. It has no impurities or additives and dissolves easily. You will need to use about half again more kosher salt than you would table salt.

Measuring cups that come with various brands of cookers differ somewhat in size but they usually have a capacity of about 6 fluid ounces. They are meant to make about the amount of rice for 1 portion. Please note that all measurements in this book are given in standard 8 oz. cups.

If the rice cooker shuts off before the food is totally cooked, add more water and start the cooker again.

The best way to clean the cooker pan is to fill it with warm soapy water and allow it to soak for a few minutes, and then use a plastic spoon or scrubber to loosen any adhering rice. Do not place the inner pan in the dishwasher. The new nonstick-lined pans clean very easily by hand.

Unlike most appliances, some rice cookers do not have an "on-off" switch, and must be unplugged to be totally off. Many have a pilot lamp to warn you that they are still on, but always remember to unplug the cooker after you have removed the food from it.

SAFETY CONSIDERATIONS

As with any appliance, there are things that one should keep constantly in mind.

1. RICE COOKERS COOK AT VERY HIGH TEMPERATURES AND WILL PRODUCE LARGE AMOUNTS OF STEAM. USE EXTREME CAUTION WHEN OPENING RICE COOKERS BOTH DURING THE COOKING CYCLE AND AFTER THE COOKING CYCLE. When lifting a detachable cover, always lift it away from your face and arms. Steam can cause serious burns. The hinged cover will spring open at the touch of a button and it is important to avert your face and quickly move your hands to avoid the steam.

2. Don't allow the cooker cord to hang over the counter edge. A child could pull the cooker off; or even brushing against the cord could pull a boiling pot off the counter and cause a serious burn.

3. If a recipe calls for the sautéeing of butter or oil, use extreme caution, as you would when cooking with other high-temperature devices like a stove or oven. The inner pot will be hot, so use a long-handled plastic spoon for stirring. DO NOT USE the short handled rice paddle for this type of cooking.

4. It is important to remember that the cooking cycle of rice cookers is controlled by the temperature of the inner pot. When liquid boils off, the temperature will rise, causing the rice cooker to automatically shift into a low temperature 'keep warm' mode. This is fine for making rice dishes but if a recipe calls for steaming or making soups, where copious quanitities of liquid are used, the rice cooker will not shut off until all liquid is boiled away. Follow the recipes carefully and do not leave the rice cooker unattended as it will contine to cook at high temperatures when making soups, stews and steaming. Monitor the cooking process and MANUALLY TURN OFF the rice cooker when the time that the recipe stipulates has elapsed.

BASIC INGREDIENTS FOR THE RICE COOKER

LONG-GRAIN RICE

Carolina—No longer from the Carolinas, but grown in Texas, Louisiana, Arkansas and Missouri. It cooks up with firm individual grains and has a pleasant neutral taste. Mahatma is a commonly available brand.

Jasmine—From Thailand. Aromatic, but doesn't smell of flowers. The aroma is described as "earthy" or "nutty," neither of which is a perfect descriptor. Has same appearance as long-grain. Cooks up soft and tender.

Indian basmati—Grown in the Himalayan foothills. True basmati has very long, slender grains that stay separate when cooked. It is intensely fragrant and has a wonderful aroma while cooking. Basmati is the perfect accompaniment for curry, and makes wonderful pilafs. The finest basmati rices are aged for a year or two after harvest to enhance the aroma.

Texmati, Jasmati and California "basmati"—All are hybrids, with some characteristic Jasmine or basmati aroma.

Parboiled—Widely available as "converted." Specially processed to retain more vitamins and nutrients. Requires more water, and a longer cooking time than regular long-grain rice. Cooked grains are firm and stay separate.

MEDIUM-GRAIN RICE

Medium-grain rice is sold under a variety of names. The grains are about twice as long as they are round. Medium-grain rice is bland and slightly stickier than long-grain. Medium-grain rice can be used in almost any recipe that calls for long-grain. Calrose is a widely available variety. In a pinch, Calrose will even make an acceptable risotto or paella.

Arborio rice—A very special medium-grain rice imported from Italy. Used for risotto in which it is cooked until just barely done in the center of the grain, and the surface starch creates a wonderful creamy sauce. It is possible to make a delicious risotto in the rice cooker. Valencia rice from Spain that is generally used in paella is very similar to Arborio, and the two can be used interchangeably.

SHORT-GRAIN RICE

Short-grain rice is also called "**pearl rice.**" Cooks up soft and sticky. This is the rice used to make sushi and rice pudding. Short-grain rice is not widely available except in Asian and Puerto Rican markets.

BROWN RICE

During the milling process, brown rice has a portion or all of the bran layer left on the rice grains. Nutritionally, brown rice has more B-complex vitamins and much more fiber than polished rice. Almost any rice type can have the bran left on the grain. The most popular brown rices are medium- and long-grain. Brown rice takes about three times as long to cook as polished rice, and the cooked rice retains a chewy texture. Since brown rice retains the germ and natural oils, it can turn stale and rancid if stored at room temperature for an extended period. Buy only what you need for a month or two. Store in an airtight container in a cool dark place to preserve maximum freshness and flavor.

EXOTIC RICES AND BLENDS

Several rice producers market special hybrid rices and blends. One of our favorites is Konriko "Wild Pecan" rice. It is neither wild rice, nor does it contain pecans. It is hybrid rice specially processed to remove about 20 percent of the bran that allows it to cook in just slightly more time than polished rice. The flavor is nutty and delicious. Lundberg Farms markets several distinctive blends of rice. We particularly like their Wild Blend, which is a combination of brown, sweet Wehani and black Japonica varieties. There are many other specialty rices available, as well as spiced and flavored rice mixes. All cook well in the rice cooker. Follow the package cooking directions.

RICE STORAGE AND COOKING

White rice will keep indefinitely if stored in an airtight container in a dark, cool place. Brown rice has a limited storage life, so buy only a two or three month supply. Some people like very soft rice while others prefer individual gains with some resistance to the bite. The softness of rice cooked in the rice cooker can be controlled by the amount of water added. Start out following package directions, and adjust the water to your taste. When the amount of rice is doubled, it isn't necessary to double the water. About two-thirds more is usually adequate. Salt the cooking water, if desired. About $\frac{1}{2}$ tsp. of salt for each cup of uncooked rice is a good starting place. If the rice is to be served plain, 1 tbs. of butter or olive oil added to the cooking water for each cup of rice will give the rice a nice silky texture and will help to keep the grains more separate. When the cooker shuts off, fluff up the rice with a fork and immediately replace the cooker cover. Allow to stand for 10 minutes more for perfect rice.

NONSTICK COOKING SPRAY

There are many nonstick cooking sprays on the market, and many other vegetable and olive oil sprays available. All do an excellent job, adding few calories. Spraying the rice cooker container with these sprays makes cleanup a much easier task, particularly because you don't want to use an abrasive scrubber on the special finish of the rice cooking pan.

STOCKS AND BROTHS

A stock or broth adds flavor, improves texture and provides some nutritional benefits to recipes, particularly soups and dishes based on rice or grain. Dishes cooked in a rice cooker do not have the benefit of the long simmering or braising that it takes to develop a flavorful broth. The best purchased stocks are sold in cans — often containing just the right amount needed to cook 1 cup of rice! We prefer to use the low or reduced sodium varieties. Also available are bouillon cubes in a wide variety of flavors. One cube and 1 cup of water usually makes 1 cup of stock.

CHINESE RESTAURANT-STYLE RICE

Servings: 3–4

The Chinese prefer rice that is not as sticky as Japanese rice but they still want a rice that is easily eaten with chopsticks. Chinese restaurants often cook a blend of rices, which is a mixture of long-grain, medium-grain and jasmine rices. The long-grain is for texture, the jasmine provides fragrance, and the medium-grain holds the cooked rice together so that it may be more easily eaten with chopsticks. Chinese restaurants rarely salt steamed rice while it cooks. The rice serves as a foil for the savory, salty dishes that are served with it. A blend that works well for us is:

1/2 cup long-grain rice
1/4 cup jasmine rice
1/4 cup medium-grain rice

Add rice to cooker pan and wash well in three or four changes of water. Then drain well. Add 1 3/4 cup cooking water and salt if desired. If you have time, allow rice to soak for 15 minutes before turning on cooker. When cooker shuts off, fluff up the rice with a fork, replace cover, and allow rice to stand for 10 minutes before serving.

SAN ANTONIO RICE

Stir a jar of your favorite fresh salsa into the rice cooker, add rice and some fresh corn kernels, and you have a flavorful supper or side dish for grilled chicken or fish.

1 cup uncooked long-grain rice
1 jar (12 oz.) fresh salsa, mild or hot
1 tbs. vegetable oil
1 cup fresh or canned corn kernels
$^1/_2$ tsp. cumin
$^1/_2$ tsp. salt
freshly ground black pepper to taste
$1^1/_4$ cups water
minced fresh cilantro for garnish, optional

Add all ingredients except cilantro to the rice cooker container, stir, cover and cook. When rice cooker switches to "keep warm" mode, open the cooker, quickly stir and re-cover. Allow to stand for 8 to 10 minutes before serving. Spoon onto a serving dish, garnish with fresh cilantro and serve.

THAI-STYLE RICE

Make this rice to serve with spicy foods. The coconut milk adds flavor and richness.

1 cup long-grain Jasmine rice
2 cups canned coconut milk
$1/4$ tsp. ground cardamom
$1/2$ tsp. ground coriander
$1/4$ tsp. salt
ribbons of fresh basil leaves or cilantro leaves for garnish, optional

Add all ingredients to the rice cooker container except basil or cilantro. Cover and cook until rice cooker shuts off, about 20 minutes. Allow to stand 10 minutes before serving.

BASIC COOKED WILD RICE

Yield: 3 to 3½ cups cooked rice

Wild rice isn't really rice, but a grass that grows in parts of the U.S. and Canada. For cooking time, rely on package instructions. Note that darker rice may take almost 1 hour to cook; brown hued wild rice may be done in 30 minutes; and "blonde" rice in about 15 minutes.

1 cup wild rice
½ tsp. salt

3½ to 4 cups chicken broth or water

Place rice in a sieve and rinse well under running water. Add to the rice cooker container with salt. Rice can be cooked in either broth or water. We prefer a light chicken or vegetable broth. If you are using a salted broth, reduce or eliminate salt. Start with 4 cups of liquid for the darker colored rices, and a little less for the brown ones. Turn on the rice cooker, cover and allow to cook for about ½ to ⅔ of expected cooking time. Carefully open cooker and look at grains. When grains have started to "bloom," showing a little white on the ends, rice is almost cooked. Taste a grain. If rice still has a slight crunch, re-cover rice cooker and allow to cook for another 10 minutes. Test again. When most of the grains have bloomed and grains are tender but still a little chewy, turn off rice cooker and allow rice to stand for a few minutes. Cool and use as directed in recipes.

ORANGE RICE PILAF

This is a delicious accompaniment for almost any fish, chicken or pork dish.

2 tbs. unsalted butter
1/4 cup onion, finely chopped, or 1 tbs. dried onion flakes
grated zest of 1 orange
juice of 2 oranges plus enough chicken broth to make 1 3/4 cups liquid
1 cup long-grain rice
1/2 tsp. kosher salt
1/4 cup slivered toasted almonds for garnish

Add all ingredients to rice cooker container except toasted almonds. Cover and cook until liquid evaporates, about 20 minutes. Allow to stand for 10 minutes. Spoon into a serving bowl, top with toasted almonds and serve immediately.

RISI E BISI (RICE WITH PEAS, HAM AND CHIVES)

Servings: 4

This traditional Italian dish is a tasty accompaniment to roast chicken and grilled fish. Double the recipe for serving as part of a buffet: spoon the cooked rice into radicchio cups or hollowed-out tomatoes and place on a platter.

2 tbs. unsalted butter
1¾ cups low sodium chicken broth
1 cup long-grain rice
¼ cup dry white wine
2 tbs. dried minced onion
½ tsp. dried thyme, or 1 tsp. fresh thyme
  leaves

kosher salt and white pepper to taste
1½ cups frozen peas, rinsed with cold water
¼ cup diced smoked ham or prosciutto,
  optional
1 tsp. minced chives, dried or fresh
grated Parmesan cheese, optional

Melt butter in the rice cooker container. Add all ingredients except peas, ham, chives and Parmesan. Cover and allow to cook until rice cooker shuts off. Carefully open the cover and stir rice. Add peas, diced ham and chives. Cover and allow to stand for 10 minutes. Serve immediately with grated Parmesan cheese, if desired.

QUICK MUSHROOM HERB RICE

"Wild Pecan" rice has more pecan aroma than taste, and is a great Southern product. Substitute 1 cup long-grain brown rice for the Wild Pecan rice if not available.

2½ cups water
1 box (7 oz.) "Wild Pecan" rice
2 tbs. unsalted butter
1 can (4 oz.) mushroom slices and pieces with juice
2 tbs. dried parsley
1 tbs. dried celery flakes
1 tbs. dried minced onion
freshly ground black pepper to taste
1 tsp. kosher salt, or ¾ tsp. regular salt
several drops red pepper sauce, or to taste

Pour water into the rice cooker container and add remaining ingredients; stir gently to combine. Cover and cook until rice cooker turns off. Carefully open lid, stir and replace cover. Allow to stand for 10 to 15 minutes before serving. Stir well and spoon into a serving dish. Serve immediately.

MADRAS CINNAMON SCENTED RICE WITH LENTILS

Servings: 3–4

The pretty pink colored dal, or split lentils, found in markets that sell ethnic foods, are combined with rice and spices for a tasty dish. If you have leftovers, use them to stuff hollowed-out fresh tomatoes, and steam for 5 minutes to heat through.

1/2 cup dal, picked over and washed
2 tbs. extra virgin olive oil
1 cup medium-grain rice
2 1/2 cups low sodium vegetable or chicken broth
2 tbs. dried minced onion
1/4 tsp. granulated garlic
2 tbs. dried parsley

1 tsp. cinnamon
1/2 tsp. cumin
1/4 tsp. crushed red pepper flakes
kosher salt and freshly ground black pepper
2 tomatoes, peeled, seeded, chopped, for garnish, or 1 cup drained canned tomato pieces
fresh cilantro for garnish, optional

Add all ingredients to the rice cooker container except tomatoes and cilantro garnish. Cover and cook until rice cooker shuts off. Carefully remove the cover, stir and re-cover. Allow to stand for another 10 minutes before serving. Place in a serving bowl, garnish with tomato and cilantro and serve immediately.

LEMON DILL RICE

This lemony rice is a delicious accompaniment for fish and chicken dishes. The lemon and herbs cook with the rice. Add shrimp or scallops and frozen peas during the last five minutes of cooking to make a main dish.

1 cup long-grain jasmine rice
1¾ cups water
½ tsp. salt
grated zest of 1 lemon
1 tbs. lemon juice
½ tsp. dried dill weed
1 tsp. dried parsley, or 1 tbs. minced fresh flat-leaf parsley
2 tbs. butter, cut into 4 pieces
kosher salt and freshly ground black pepper to taste

Add all ingredients to the rice cooker container. Stir to combine. Cover and cook until rice cooker shuts off. Allow rice to stand, covered, for 10 minutes. Adjust seasoning. Pour into a serving bowl and serve immediately.

SAVORY LENTILS

Lentils, like rice and pasta, provide a wonderful base for almost any combination of spices and flavors. This is a quick and easy side dish. **NOTE:** *When sautéeing butter or oil, use extreme caution, as you would when cooking with other high-temperature devices like a stove or oven. The inner pot will be hot, so use a long-handled wooden spoon for stirring. DO NOT USE the short handled rice paddle for this type of cooking.*

2 tbs. extra virgin olive oil
1/2 tsp. curry powder
1 tsp. cumin
1 cup brown or green lentils, picked over
   and washed
2 2/3 cups water

1 can (14 oz.) tomato pieces with juice
2 tbs. dried minced onion
1 tbs. dried vegetable flakes
2 tbs. dried parsley
kosher salt and freshly ground black pepper
   to taste

Add all ingredients, stir, cover and cook until rice cooker shuts off. Midway through cooking, carefully open rice cooker and stir ingredients. Stir again when cooker shuts off, close cover and allow lentils to stand for 10 minutes before serving.

BASMATI RICE AND CORN SALAD

Domestically grown basmati does not need to be rinsed in several changes of water, but allowing it to soak for 15 minutes before cooking helps keep the grains separate when cooked.

1 cup basmati rice
1³/₄ cups water
³/₄ tsp. kosher salt, or ¹/₂ tsp. regular salt
2 cups fresh or frozen corn kernels
2 tbs. red wine vinegar
1 tbs. Dijon-style mustard

¹/₃ cup extra virgin olive oil
¹/₂ cup crumbled cooked bacon
5–6 green onions, white part with 1 inch of
  green, thinly sliced
kosher salt and freshly ground black pepper
2 tbs. chopped flat-leaf parsley for garnish

Add rice, water and salt to the rice cooker container. Soak rice for 15 minutes before turning on cooker. Cover and cook rice until cooker shuts off. Stir in corn, re-cover, and allow to stand for 10 minutes. Pour rice and corn into a large bowl and fluff mixture with a fork.

In a small bowl, whisk together vinegar and mustard, add olive oil and whisk well. Pour dressing over rice and toss gently to combine. Add bacon, green onions and salt and pepper to taste. Sprinkle parsley over salad just before serving. Serve at room temperature.

Variation: Substitute ²/₃ cup toasted pecan pieces or slivered almonds for bacon.

DELI RICE SALAD

Make this salad 1 to 2 hours before serving so flavors have time to marry. This is a great lunch or picnic treat. It assembles quickly with cooked rice and pick-up items from the deli.

2 cups cooked long-grain rice
1/2 cup drained and rinsed kidney or
   garbanzo beans
4 oz. salami or smoked ham, cut in slivers
4 oz. smoked Gouda or Provolone, cut in
   small dice

2 tbs. finely chopped red onion
1 medium dill pickle, finely chopped
2 tbs. finely chopped fresh flat-leaf parsley
1/4 tsp. crushed red pepper flakes
kosher salt and freshly ground black pepper
   to taste

VINAIGRETTE

1/4 cup extra virgin olive oil
2 tbs. cider vinegar
1 tbs. Dijon-style mustard

1/4 tsp. dried oregano
1/4 tsp. dried basil
kosher salt and freshly ground black pepper

Combine salad ingredients in a large bowl. Whisk vinaigrette until well combined, pour over salad and toss using two forks. If refrigerating, bring to room temperature before serving.

SAN JUAN BLACK BEAN AND RICE SALAD

This hearty salad includes flavors of the Caribbean. If queso fresco (Mexican style fresh cheese) is not available, crumbled feta is a nonauthentic but delicious substitute. Serve with a fresh fruit platter of melon, mango and pineapple slices.

2 cups cooked medium-grain rice
1 can (15 oz.) black beans, drained and
   rinsed
1/4 cup diced roasted red peppers

6–8 black kalamata olives, pitted and
   chopped
3 oz. queso fresco or feta cheese, crumbled
minced fresh cilantro leaves for garnish

DRESSING
1/4 cup extra virgin olive oil
1 tbs. red wine vinegar
1 tbs. lemon juice

1 tbs. Dijon-style mustard
kosher salt and generous amounts freshly
   ground black pepper to taste

Place rice, beans, red peppers and olive pieces in a serving bowl and stir to combine. Whisk dressing ingredients together in a small bowl and toss with rice. Sprinkle with cheese and fresh cilantro. Serve at room temperature.

NEW POTATOES WITH SMOKED SALMON SALAD

Small new potatoes and smoked salmon dressed with dill and yogurt make a nice first course or luncheon salad.

12 oz. *Steamed New Potatoes,* unpeeled (see page 47)
1 tbs. sweet-hot mustard
2 tbs plain yogurt
½ tsp. dried dill, or 1 tbs. chopped fresh
1 tbs. minced fresh flat-leaf parsley
kosher salt and freshly ground black pepper to taste
1–2 oz. thinly sliced smoked salmon, cut into 1-inch squares

When potatoes are cool enough to handle, slice each into quarters and place in a bowl. In a small bowl, mix together sweet-hot mustard, yogurt, dill and parsley. Gently toss with potatoes; season with salt and pepper to taste. Stir in smoked salmon pieces. Refrigerate until ready to serve. This can be made a day ahead.

EASY GINGERED CARROT ORANGE SOUP

This dramatic soup can be served hot or cold, and freezes well. Push the finished soup through a coarse strainer for an extra silky finish if serving cold. Serve in glass bowls or teacups. **NOTE:** *Monitor the cooking process and MANUALLY TURN OFF the rice cooker when the time that the recipe stipulates has elapsed.*

2 tbs. unsalted butter
1 small onion, thinly sliced
1 lb.carrots, coarsely shredded
1 tsp. finely minced fresh ginger
$1/8$ tsp. crushed red pepper flakes

3 cups chicken broth, see page 12
1 tbs. grated orange zest
$1\frac{1}{4}$ cups orange juice
kosher salt and finely ground white pepper
minced flat leaf parsley or chives for garnish

Turn on the rice cooker and add butter to the container. When butter is foaming, add onions, carrots and ginger. Cook for 5 to 6 minutes until vegetables soften, stirring occasionally. Add chicken broth and orange zest. Re-cover and cook for 20 minutes, until carrots and onions are very soft. Turn off cooker and allow mixture to cool for a few minutes. Add orange juice to carrots and carefully transfer mixture in 2 or 3 small batches to a blender or food processor. Process until smooth. Return soup to rice cooker container and reheat before serving. If serving chilled, pour into a large bowl, cover and refrigerate for several hours.

EASY BLACK AND WHITE BEAN SOUP

*Diced cooked ham, chicken or any type of cooked sausage can be substituted for linguiça. Drain and discard the black bean juice as it will make the finished soup look murky. **NOTE:** When sautéeing, use extreme caution. The inner pot will be hot, so use a long-handled wooden spoon for stirring. DO NOT USE the short handled rice paddle for this type of cooking.*

1 tbs. extra virgin olive oil
$\frac{1}{2}$ cup finely chopped onion
$\frac{1}{2}$ tsp. sambal oelek (a mixture of chiles, brown
   sugar and salt) or chile paste with garlic
1 cup diced cooked linguiça
2 cups chicken broth, see page 12
1 can (15$\frac{1}{2}$ oz.) diced tomatoes with juice

1 can (15 oz.) small white or cannellini
   beans, with juice
1 can (15 oz.) black beans, drained, juice
   discarded
kosher salt and freshly ground black pepper
$\frac{1}{4}$ cup chopped fresh cilantro or parsley for
   garnish

Heat oil in the rice cooker container and add onions and sausage. Cook for 3 to 4 minutes, stirring occasionally. Add chicken broth, tomatoes and sambal oelek. Cover and cook for 15 minutes. Add beans and continue to cook for 5 minutes. Turn cooker off. Adjust seasoning. Serve immediately in warmed soup bowls and garnish with cilantro.

Note: Crushed red pepper flakes can be substituted for the sambal oelek.

POTATO AND LEEK SOUP

This classic soup cooks quickly in the rice cooker. It can be served hot or used as the base to make a cold Vichyssoise.

2 large leeks, white part only, thinly sliced
2 tbs. unsalted butter
1 medium stalk celery, thinly sliced
2 large baking potatoes, about 10 oz. each,
   peeled, thinly sliced

4 cups chicken or vegetable broth, see page
   12
½ tsp. kosher salt
ground white pepper to taste
minced chives or flat-leaf parsley for garnish

Place sliced leeks in a strainer and wash under running cold water to remove any sand. Pat dry on paper towels. Melt butter in the rice cooker container, add leeks and celery, and cook, uncovered, for 4 to 5 minutes, until vegetables soften. Stir occasionally. Add potatoes and chicken broth, then cover and cook for 20 minutes, until vegetables are tender. Turn off cooker and allow soup to cool for a few minutes. Transfer potato mixture in 2 or 3 small batches to a blender or food processor and process until smooth. Adjust seasoning. Serve soup hot in warmed soup bowls and garnish with chives or parsley.

Vichyssoise variation: Combine 2 cups of potato and leek soup with ½ cup heavy cream. Cover and chill for several hours. Serve cold, garnished with chives.

GREEN CHILE AND CHICKEN RICE

Servings: 4

All you need is a can opener for this quick main course.

1½ cups medium-grain rice, such as Calrose
3 cups low sodium chicken broth
2 tbs. dried minced onion
½ tsp. kosher salt
1 can (10 oz.) chicken breast chunks with liquid
1 can (4 oz.) diced green chiles with liquid
salt to taste

Place all ingredients in the rice cooker container and stir. Cover and cook until rice cooker shuts off. Add salt to your taste. Stir and serve immediately.

SAVORY SAUSAGE AND RICE

This is a favorite rainy night dinner. Serve with a crisp green salad, garlic bread, and a red zinfandel wine.

1 cup uncooked long-grain rice
1 pkg. (2 oz.) chicken noodle soup mix
3½ cups water
1 lb. mild or hot bulk sausage
1 cup chopped onion
1 fresh red or green pepper, peeled, diced

1 tbs. dried parsley, or 2 tbs. chopped fresh
   flat-leaf parsley
2 tomatoes, peeled, seeded, chopped
kosher salt and freshly ground black pepper
   to taste
grated Parmesan cheese

Add rice, chicken noodle soup mix and water to the rice cooker container. Cover and cook until rice cooker shuts off. While rice is cooking, brown sausage in a nonstick skillet, crumbling into small pieces as it cooks. Remove sausage to a strainer and drain. Return about 2 tbs. of the sausage drippings to skillet. Sauté onion and red pepper for 5 to 6 minutes, until soft but not browned. When rice cooker turns off, carefully remove cover and quickly stir in cooked meat, onion mixture, parsley and tomatoes. Cover and allow to stand for 10 minutes. Spoon into a warm serving bowl and serve immediately. Pass Parmesan cheese if desired.

RICE WITH LENTILS

The brown lentils take longer to cook than rice, so they are started a few minutes before adding rice. Serve with a fresh fruit or green salad, crisp cheese bread and a red zinfandel.
NOTE: *Rice cookers cook at very high temperatures and produce large amounts of steam. Use extreme caution when opening the cooker, both during and after the cooking cycle.*

$\frac{1}{2}$ cup lentils, picked over and washed
2 tbs. extra virgin olive oil
3 cups beef or chicken broth
2 tbs. dried minced onion
$\frac{1}{2}$ tsp. granulated garlic
2 tbs. dried parsley
1 cup medium-grain rice

$\frac{1}{2}$ tsp. kosher salt
1 tsp. ground cumin
$\frac{1}{4}$ tsp. crushed red pepper flakes
$\frac{1}{4}$ cup diced sun-dried tomatoes
1 medium-size tomato, peeled, seeded, chopped, for garnish
2 tbs. chopped fresh flat-leaf parsley

Add lentils, olive oil and broth to the rice cooker container. Cover and cook for 15 minutes. Add remaining ingredients, except tomato pieces and parsley, and continue to cook until rice cooker shuts off. Carefully remove cover, quickly stir and re-cover. Allow to stand for 10 minutes before serving. Spoon into a serving bowl and top with chopped tomato and parsley. Serve immediately.

JAMBALAYA

Try making this classic Louisiana dish with leftover cooked chicken or ham—or add a few shrimp during the last minutes of steaming. **NOTE:** *When sautéeing, use extreme caution. The inner pot will be hot, so use a long-handled wooden spoon for stirring. DO NOT USE the short handled rice paddle for this.*

2 tbs. extra virgin olive oil
1 cup coarsely chopped onion
1 red bell pepper, peeled and diced
1 medium stalk celery, diced
1 cup uncooked long-grain rice
1 3/4 cups chicken broth
1 can (14 oz.) tomato pieces with juice
1 tbs. tomato paste
1/2 tsp. dried thyme

3/4 tsp. kosher salt, or 1/2 tsp. regular salt
freshly ground black pepper to taste
1 pinch powdered cloves
1/4 tsp. prepared chili powder
1 tbs. dried parsley
6–8 drops Tabasco Sauce
1/3 cup diced ham
6 oz. smoked Polish sausage, cut into slices
6–8 medium shrimp, optional

Heat oil in the rice cooker container and sauté onion, pepper and celery for 3 to 4 minutes to soften. Add rice and stir to coat. Add remaining ingredients. Cover and cook, stirring once or twice, until rice cooker turns off. Allow jambalaya to stand for about 10 minutes before serving on warmed plates.

QUICK FRIED RICE

Cold cooked rice is a must for good fried rice. Basmati rice is particularly good in this dish. Roll rice clumps between your fingers to break them into individual grains. For variation, use leftover cooked asparagus or broccoli instead of peas.

3 tbs. vegetable oil

4 green onions, white part and 2 inches of green, thinly sliced

3 cups cold cooked rice, crumbled

2 large eggs, lightly beaten

$1/2$ cup diced cooked ham, chicken, sausage or shrimp

$1/2$ cup frozen green peas, rinsed with cold water

2 tbs. soy sauce

1 tsp. toasted sesame oil

$1/8$ tsp. ground white pepper

fresh chopped cilantro leaves for garnish

Heat vegetable oil in a wok or a large nonstick skillet. Sauté onions for 1 to 2 minutes to soften. Add crumbled rice and cook for 3 to 4 minutes over medium heat, stirring constantly. Make a well in middle of rice and pour in beaten eggs. When eggs start to set, stir into rice, breaking into small pieces. Add ham, peas, soy sauce and sesame oil. Season with pepper and continue to cook for 1 minute, until mixture is hot. Garnish with cilantro and serve in a warm bowl or on warm plates.

SHRIMP WITH SAFFRON RICE

A small amount of saffron adds a unique flavor and color to rice. Turmeric can be substituted to produce the color if not the flavor. The rice is timed to cook for a few minutes, then the shrimp are added for the last few minutes of cooking. Do not allow rice to stand after rice cooker shuts off because shrimp will be overcooked. Jasmine rice is a good choice for this dish.

1 cup jasmine or long-grain rice
1 cup low sodium chicken broth
1 bottle (8 oz.) clam juice, or 1 cup water
2 tbs. unsalted butter
1 tbs. dried minced onion
zest of 1 lemon
2 tbs. lemon juice

generous pinch saffron, or $1/4$ tsp. turmeric
5–6 drops Tabasco Sauce, or to taste
kosher salt and freshly ground black pepper
   to taste
8 oz. large shrimp, peeled, de-veined, tails
   left on
fresh or dried minced chives for garnish

Place all ingredients except shrimp and chives in the rice cooker container. After liquid starts to boil, cook rice for 10 minutes. Carefully open rice cooker and add shrimp on top of rice. Cover and continue to cook until rice cooker shuts off. Serve immediately and garnish with chives.

BASQUE-STYLE RICE AND CLAMS

Serve with a crisp salad, or fill individual clam shells or au gratin dishes for a first course. Fresh clams make an attractive garnish but the dish is delicious without them.

2 cans (6½ oz. each) chopped clams with juice
1 bottle (8 oz.) clam juice
3 tbs. extra virgin olive oil
½ cup chopped onion
2 cloves garlic, minced
1 cup uncooked medium-grain rice
⅓ cup finely chopped fresh flat-leaf parsley
1 large tomato, peeled, seeded, chopped
1 pinch saffron threads, optional
¾ tsp. kosher salt, or ½ tsp. regular salt
6–8 fresh clams in shells, scrubbed, optional
1 dash red pepper flakes
½ cup diced cooked ham or frozen green peas

Drain clams and strain juice through a coffee filter or cheesecloth to catch any sand. Reserve juice. Combine reserved clam juice with bottle of clam juice, plus enough water to make 2¼ cups total liquid. With lid closed, heat olive oil in rice cooker container. When hot, sauté onions and garlic, with lid closed, over low heat for 3 to 4 minutes, to soften onion. Pour in clam juice with water, rice, onion, parsley, tomato, saffron, salt, fresh clams (if using) and red pepper flakes. Cover and cook until liquid evaporates and rice cooker turns off. Immediately lift lid, remove cooked clams in the shell, and quickly stir in chopped clams, ham or peas and red pepper strips. Cover and allow to stand for an additional 10 minutes. Serve immediately on warmed plates. Garnish with whole clams in shell.

Variation: To serve as a first course, fill individual ovenproof serving dishes with rice and clam mixture. Sprinkle with buttered fresh breadcrumbs or Parmesan cheese. Place under broiler for a few minutes to brown lightly. Makes 6 to 8 first course servings.

TUNA AND SPINACH RICE

Everyone has a favorite tuna and rice dish. Sprinkle with finely grated cheddar cheese just before serving, if you like that combination.

1 cup long-grain rice
2 cups water
1 tbs. dried minced onion
$1/2$ tsp. kosher salt
freshly ground black pepper to taste
1 can ($6^1/2$ oz.) tuna packed in oil, drained, oil reserved
1 tsp. grated lemon zest
1 pkg. (10 oz.) creamed spinach, defrosted
cheddar cheese, optional

Add rice, water, onion, salt, pepper and oil from tuna to the rice cooker container. Stir, cover and cook until rice cooker shuts off. Carefully open rice cooker and stir in tuna, lemon zest, and creamed spinach. Re-cover and allow to stand for 10 minutes before serving. Top with grated cheddar cheese, if desired.

CHINESE-STYLE STEAMED ROCK COD

Almost any firm-fleshed fish (like red snapper, sea bass or halibut fillets) can be used here.

2 rock cod fillets, about 4–6 oz. each
1 tbs. soy sauce
1/4 tsp. toasted sesame oil
1 small clove garlic, minced
1 tsp. fresh ginger, minced
1 pinch white pepper

1 tbs. rice wine vinegar
2 green onions, white part with 1 inch of
    green, slivered
5–6 slivered snow peas
fresh cilantro leaves

Choose a plate that will allow about 1/2-inch circulation around it in the rice cooker container. Spray plate with nonstick spray. Place 2 fish fillets on the plate. Fold thin parts of fish under to make more uniform pieces. Mix together soy sauce, sesame oil, garlic, ginger, white pepper and rice wine vinegar. Pour over fish fillets. Top with slivered onions and snow peas. Cover plate with plastic wrap and place in steamer tray. Add 1 cup water to rice cooker container, cover and bring to a boil. Carefully open cooker and add steamer tray. Cover and steam for about 7 to 8 minutes. The fish is done when it flakes or feels firm to the touch. Do not overcook. Carefully remove steamer tray from rice cooker. Place fish on warmed serving plates. Garnish with fresh cilantro leaves. Serve immediately.

SHRIMP COOKED IN BEER

This is an easy dish for informal entertaining. If you have any shrimp left over, refrigerate and eat them for lunch the next day. Choose a pilsner or light beer for steaming liquid.

1 lb. medium-size shrimp in the shell
12 oz. pilsner or light beer
1 pinch crushed red pepper flakes
kosher salt

With scissors, cut shrimp shells down the back and pull off the legs. Lift out the dark vein with a toothpick and rinse with water. Place shrimp in rice cooker container and pour in enough beer to just cover shrimp. Add red pepper flakes and 1 pinch salt. Bring beer to a boil. Uncover to stir once or twice. Shrimp are done when they turn a bright pink, about 3 to 4 minutes after beer comes to a boil. Immediately pour shrimp into a strainer and then into a serving bowl. Serve warm, cold or at room temperature with lots of napkins, a bowl for shells and aioli or cocktail sauce.

ARROZ CON POLLO

Succulent morsels of chicken are cooked with rice and spices to make a delicious supper or hearty lunch. Dried herbs and vegetables make this dish quick to prepare. **NOTE:** *Monitor the cooking process and MANUALLY TURN OFF the rice cooker when the time that the recipe stipulates has elapsed.*

6 boneless, skinless chicken thighs, cut into
  1-inch pieces
3 tbs. extra virgin olive oil
1 red bell pepper, peeled, seeded, chopped
1½ cups medium-grain rice
2 tbs. dried minced onion
1 tsp. granulated garlic
1 tbs. dried parsley

2 tsp. Spanish paprika
3 cups low sodium chicken broth
1½ cups canned tomato pieces with juice
½ tsp. Tabasco Sauce
kosher salt and freshly ground black pepper
  to taste
1 pinch saffron, optional

Heat olive oil in rice cooker container and sauté chicken pieces for 2 to 3 minutes. Add red pepper and rice, and stir to coat rice with the oil. Add remaining ingredients, stir, cover and cook until rice cooker shuts off. Carefully remove cover and stir rice. Re-cover and allow to stand for 10 minutes before serving on warmed plates.

BASIC STEAMED CHICKEN BREASTS

This basic steamed chicken breast recipe is great for salads and sandwiches. It is also good in soups.

2 boneless, skinless chicken breasts
kosher salt and freshly ground black pepper to taste

Choose a plate that is just large enough to fit into the rice cooker tray with about $1/2$-inch clearance for steam circulation. Spray plate with nonstick spray. Place chicken breasts on plate and season with salt and pepper. Cover plate with plastic wrap.

Add 1 cup water to rice cooker container, cover and bring to a boil. Carefully open cooker and add steamer tray. Cover and steam for about 10 minutes, until chicken is firm to the touch. Carefully remove tray from rice cooker, remove plastic wrap, and serve.

SOY SAUCE-MARINATED CHICKEN BREASTS

Boneless, skinless chicken breasts or turkey cutlets are marinated and cooked in an Asian flavored sauce.

2 boneless, skinless chicken breasts or turkey breast cutlets, about $3/4$-inch thick
2 tbs. soy sauce
1 tbs. sugar
1 tsp. toasted sesame oil
1 small clove garlic, minced
$1/2$ tsp. grated fresh ginger
1 green onion, white part with 1 inch of green, cut into slivers

Combine soy sauce, sugar, sesame oil, garlic and ginger with chicken breasts and marinate for 10 to 15 minutes. Place chicken breasts and marinade on a plate sprayed with nonstick cooking spray, top with slivered onion, and cover plate with plastic wrap. Steam as directed for *Basic Steamed Chicken Breasts*, page 40.

Serve chicken breasts on plates with a spoonful of marinade.

CHICKEN BREASTS WITH WINE AND SHALLOTS

Servings: 2

Boneless chicken breasts make a fast and savory dinner entrée.

2 boneless, skinless chicken breasts
2 tbs. unsalted butter
1 tbs. minced shallots
¼ cup dry white wine
kosher salt and freshly ground black pepper to taste
1 dash Tabasco Sauce
1 tomato, peeled, seeded, chopped
5–6 basil leaves, cut into thin shreds

Place boneless chicken breasts on a plate sprayed with nonstick cooking spray. In a small skillet, melt butter and sauté shallots for 1 to 2 minutes to soften. Pour in white wine, turn heat to high and reduce for 1 minute. Pour shallot mixture over chicken and cover with plastic wrap. Plase plate in steamer tray. Steam as directed for *Basic Steamed Chicken Breasts,* page 40. Remove chicken breasts to warmed plates and garnish with tomato pieces and shredded basil leaves.

CHICKEN BREASTS DIJON

A simple marinade of Dijon-style mustard and yogurt makes a quick savory entrée. This makes a delicious hot toasted sandwich, as well. Chili bean paste with garlic can be substituted for the sambal oelek.

2 boneless, skinless chicken breasts
1 tbs. Dijon-style mustard
1 tbs. plain yogurt
$\frac{1}{2}$ tsp. sambal oelek (a mixture of chiles, brown sugar and salt), optional
kosher salt and freshly ground black pepper to taste
1 tsp. dried chives

Place chicken breasts on a small plate sprayed with nonstick spray. Mix together mustard, yogurt, sambal oelek, salt and pepper. Spread over chicken breasts and sprinkle with chives. Cover chicken on plate with plastic wrap and place plate in steamer tray. Steam as directed for *Basic Steamed Chicken Breasts,* page 40. Carefully remove steamer tray from rice cooker and remove plastic wrap. Place chicken breasts on warmed serving plates. Serve immediately.

STEAMED TURKEY TENDERLOINS

Cooked turkey tenderloins make great sandwiches and salads. They steam in about 25 minutes and can be done ahead and refrigerated. A general rule is to stand for 15 minutes per 1-inch thickness. After the tenderloins have cooled, slice thinly and serve with tuna mayonnaise or salsa verde, as part of a luncheon or salad buffet.

2 turkey tenderloins, about 10–11 oz. each
kosher salt and freshly ground black pepper to taste

Add 3 cups of water to rice cooker container and bring to a boil. Season tenderloins with salt and pepper. Choose a plate that is just large enough to fit into the rice cooker tray with about 1/2-inch clearance for steam circulation. Spray plate with nonstick spray. Place tenderloins in one layer on plate, cover with plastic wrap and place in steamer tray. Carefully place steamer tray into rice cooker container, cover and steam tenderloins for about 25 minutes. Check after 20 minutes with an instant meat thermometer. Turkey should reach about 160°, and not be pink in the center. Remove from cooker and refrigerate if not serving immediately.

STEAMED ARTICHOKES

Steamed artichokes are a snap in the rice cooker. The size of your cooking container will limit the number of artichokes you can place in one layer and cook at the same time. 8 ounce artichokes, about 3 inches in diameter, can stand up in the steamer tray. If artichokes are larger, lay them on their sides, or cut them in half, remove choke and steam them cut side up.

trimmed artichokes   lemon juice
3 cups water

Wash artichokes. Cut off stems and remove about 1 inch from top. Pull off 2 or 3 layers of outer leaves. Trim remaining uncut leaves straight across with scissors. Trim rough edges of artichoke bottom where leaves were removed. Sprinkle artichokes with lemon juice.

Add 3 cups of water to the rice cooker container and bring to a boil. Place trimmed whole or halved artichokes in the steamer tray and carefully put tray in the rice cooker. Cover and cook for 20 to 25 minutes, depending on size and if whole or halved. Halved artichokes will cook in about 20 minutes. Artichoke is done when bottom is easily pierced with a knife. If artichoke bottom is not tender, cover and let steam for a few more minutes. Remove artichokes from rice cooker and place on a serving platter. Serve artichokes warm or at room temperature, and dip in mayonnaise, melted butter, or dijon mustard sauce.

AROMATIC HERBED ARTICHOKES

Serve warm or cool with mayonnaise or aioli. These make delicious picnic fare.

2 artichokes, about 8 oz. each
2 tbs. extra virgin olive oil
2 tsp. lemon juice
1/4 cup dry white wine
2 tbs. finely minced onion

2 tbs. finely chopped fresh flat-leaf parsley
1/2 tsp. dried tarragon, or 2 tsp. chopped fresh
kosher salt and freshly ground black pepper

Wash artichokes and cut bottom stem flush with artichoke bottom. Cut about 1 inch off top of artichoke. Remove 2 or 3 layers of outer leaves; trim artichoke bottom and cut in half. Pull out a few of the thorny center leaves and remove choke with a sharp spoon to make a small cup for olive oil herb mixture. Gently flatten artichoke to spread leaves slightly apart. Spoon olive oil herb mixture into spread leaves and center cup of artichoke.

Add 3 cups water to the rice cooker container and bring to a boil. Choose a plate just large enough to fit into the steamer tray with about 1/2 inch for circulation. Place halved artichokes on the plate in the steamer tray and carefully put the tray in the rice cooker. Cover and steam for about 20 minutes. Artichokes are done when bottoms are easily pierced with a knife. Remove from container to serving plate.

BASIC STEAMED NEW POTATOES

Small new potatoes cook beautifully in one layer in the rice cooker.

1–2 lb. small new potatoes (about 1 to 2 inches in diameter), scrubbed, unpeeled

Add potatoes in one layer to steamer tray. Add 3 cups water to the rice cooker container, add tray, cover and cook until potatoes are tender, about 20 minutes after water starts to boil. Test potatoes: if not completely cooked, replace cover and cook for another few minutes. Serve hot with butter, salt and pepper; or in *New Potatoes with Smoked Salmon Salad*, page 24.

STEAMED SWEET POTATOES

Makes about 1 1/4 cups

Steam sweet potatoes or yams in the rice cooker steamer tray. These are great served hot with a little butter, or purée them and make a steamed sweet potato or yam pudding.

1 lb. sweet potatoes

Peel and cut potatoes into 1-inch cubes and place in a single layer in a steamer tray. Add 2 cups water to the rice cooker container, cover and bring to a boil. Carefully place steamer tray into rice cooker. Cover and cook for about 17 minutes. Test for doneness with a fork. Remove from rice cooker and serve immediately.

STEAMED GREEN BEANS

Green beans have a nice texture when steamed in the rice cooker, and are great in salads.

1 lb. green beans, stemmed

Place beans in a steamer basket. Add 2 cups of water to the rice cooker container, cover and bring to a boil. Carefully add beans to rice cooker container and cook for 10 to 12 minutes. Check to see if beans are tender. If not, continue to steam for 1 to 2 minutes longer. Carefully remove lid, place beans on platter, season with salt, pepper and butter, and serve immediately, or allow to cool for use in another recipe.

STEAMED BUTTERNUT SQUASH

Look for ready-to-cook packages of butternut squash in the supermarket. Serve tossed with butter and seasoned with salt and pepper, or drizzled with maple syrup and a pinch of cinnamon.

1 lb. butternut squash, peeled, cut into 1-inch cubes

Place squash in the steamer tray. Add 2 cups water to the rice cooker container, cover and bring to a boil. Add steamer tray to rice cooker, cover, and cook for 10 to 12 minutes, until squash is tender. Remove from cooker, season as desired, and serve.

SWEET CORN

Sweet corn steams to perfection in the rice cooker.

fresh corn, trimmed, cut in half if needed

Remove cornhusks and silk and trim as needed. Place corn ears on steamer tray. Add 1½ cups water to the rice cooker container, cover and bring to a boil. Carefully add steamer tray with corn to rice cooker, cover and cook for 10 minutes. Remove corn immediately. Season as desired and serve hot.

STEAMED BROCCOLI

Broccoli comes out of the rice cooker a pretty green color. Cook it to the texture you like.

broccoli

Cut broccoli into florets or pieces with 2 to 3 inch stems. Place on steamer tray. Add 1½ cups water to rice cooker container, cover and bring to a boil. Place steamer tray with broccoli in rice cooker container. Cover and cook for about 8 to 10 minutes, to desired crispness. Test with the tip of a knife. Remove to a serving dish. Season with salt, pepper, and a drizzle of extra virgin olive oil, if desired.

STEAMED CAULIFLOWER

Cauliflower florets steam well. After 1½ cups water come to a boil in the rice cooker. Place florets on steamer tray, and steam as for *Broccoli,* above. Grate a little sharp cheddar cheese over hot seasoned florets if desired.

MARINATED MUSHROOMS

These piquant mushrooms keep well in the refrigerator for a few days and are a delicious addition to an antipasto or salad plate.

½ lb. button mushrooms
2 tbs. extra virgin olive oil
1 tbs. lemon juice
¼ cup rice wine vinegar
¼ cup dry sherry or white wine
1 clove garlic

¼ tsp. sugar
½ tsp. dried thyme
½ tsp. dried basil
generous dash crushed red pepper flakes
kosher salt and freshly ground black pepper
    to taste

Clean mushrooms and cut stems flush with mushroom top. If mushrooms are large, cut into quarters. Add all ingredients except mushrooms to the rice cooker container. Cover and bring to a boil. Add mushrooms to boiling liquid and cook for 5 minutes. Turn off cooker and allow to cool in liquid. Pour mushrooms and liquid into a bowl, and season to taste with salt and pepper.

ORANGE GINGERED CARROTS

Carrots flavored with fresh ginger and orange are a colorful and delicious addition to any meal. If you like crisp-tender carrots, remove them when they reach the desired degree of doneness. These can also be served at room temperature.

½ lb. carrots, peeled, sliced or cut into ⅜-inch square by x 3-inch-long strips
grated zest of 1 orange
½ cup orange juice or combination orange juice and water
2 slices fresh ginger
1 tbs. butter

Add carrots and remaining ingredients to the rice cooker container. Cover and cook for 10 minutes after liquid has come to a boil. Check to see if carrots are tender. If not, cover and continue to cook for 1 to 2 minutes more, adding more water if needed. Remove from pan and serve.

STEAMED BEETS

Vivid red beets are steamed over an orange-flavored liquid that is then reduced to make a quick sauce. The beet skins slip off easily after cooking. The steamer tray works well to hold the beets.

5–6 beets, about 2 inches in diameter
grated zest and juice of 1 orange
1 tbs. rice wine vinegar

$\frac{1}{2}$ tsp. sugar
kosher salt and freshly ground black pepper
  to taste

Cut off leafy beet tops to within 1 inch of beet. Wash, taking care not to break beet skin. Arrange beets in steamer tray; add $2\frac{1}{2}$ cups water, orange zest and juice to rice cooker container. Cover and cook for about 35 to 40 minutes, depending on size of beet. When beets are tender, remove to a plate and allow to cool. Peel, cut off tops and root ends, cut into $\frac{1}{4}$-inch slices, and place in a bowl.

Add rice wine vinegar, sugar, salt and pepper to rice cooker and continue to cook for about 8 to 10 minutes, reducing liquid to $\frac{1}{3}$ cup. Taste for seasoning and add a little more vinegar and sugar if desired. Pour sauce over beets and serve warm.

DIM SUM BARBECUED CHICKEN BUNS

Flavor some cooked chicken with your favorite barbecue sauce for a tasty filling for the Chinese-style steamed buns. The bun dough is easy to make in the food processor.

1 cup cake flour
1 cup all-purpose flour
2 tbs. sugar
2½ tsp. baking powder
1 tbs. vegetable shortening
²/₃ cup milk
¾ cup cooked chicken, in ⅜-inch cubes
⅓ cup barbecue sauce

Add flours, sugar and baking powder to the food processor workbowl. Pulse 3 or 4 times to mix well. Add shortening and pulse several times to combine. With processor running, add milk and process until dough forms a ball. Turn out dough onto a lightly floured board and knead for 1 to 2 minutes. Dough will be quite soft. Form dough into a log about 12 inches long. Cover with plastic wrap and allow dough to rest while preparing filling.

Combine chicken pieces and barbecue sauce in a small saucepan. Heat through over low heat, stirring frequently so sauce doesn't stick or burn. Remove from heat and allow to cool before filling buns.

To form buns, cut dough into 8 equal pieces. Take a piece of dough and flatten into a 3- to 4-inch circle, thicker in the middle than on the edges. Put about 2 tbs. of filling in the middle of the circle and pull up sides of dough. Pleat and pinch dough to seal top. Place each bun on a 2-inch square of aluminum foil.

Add about 3 cups water to the rice cooker container, cover and bring water to a boil. Place 4 buns in steamer tray and carefully place into rice cooker container. Cover and steam for 10 minutes. Remove cooked buns with kitchen tongs and repeat steaming process with remaining 4 buns. These buns freeze well. Serve at room temperature or reheat by steaming over hot water for a few minutes.

SHAO MAI DUMPLINGS

A Cantonese dim sum is not complete without these tasty steamed dumplings. Purchase round 3-inch shao mai wrappers, or cut square won ton wrappers into 3-inch circles.

FILLING

1 dried shiitake mushroom

¼ lb. peeled, de-veined small raw shrimp

¼ lb. lean ground pork

2 tbs. peeled, finely diced water chestnut or jicama

2 green onions, white part with 1 inch of green, finely minced

1 tsp. grated fresh ginger

1 clove garlic, minced

1 tbs. oyster sauce or Worcestershire sauce

kosher salt and white pepper to taste

3-inch round shao mai wrappers

fresh cilantro leaves

SHAO MAI DIPPING SAUCE

3 tbs. soy sauce

2 tbs. rice wine vinegar

2 tsp. hot pepper oil

Cover dried mushroom with boiling water and let stand for 15 minutes to soften. Squeeze dry, cut out and discard the tough stem and finely chop the cap. If preparing by hand, all ingredients including shrimp should be finely chopped and then combined. If using the food processor, mince water chestnut, onions, ginger and garlic in food processor and then add remaining ingredients, pulsing a few times to chop fine. Do not over-process.

To assemble: Place about 1 tbs. of the mixture in center of a wrapper. Bring sides of wrapper up around filling, pleating wrapper at the edge to form a cup. The finished shao mai will look like a tiny cupcake showing meat filling in center. Place a fresh cilantro leaf over meat. Keep unused wrappers covered with a damp paper towel so they don't dry out.

To steam: Place about 2 cups water in the rice cooker container and bring to a boil. Arrange shao mai in steamer tray about 1 inch apart. When water is steaming, carefully add steamer tray to the rice cooker. Cover and steam for 15 minutes. Remove shao mai and serve immediately.

To serve: Pour a small amount of dipping sauce into small individual dishes. Dip shao mai into sauce. The cooked shao mai can be refrigerated and reheated in the microwave or steamed for a few minutes. These can also be assembled ahead, covered with plastic wrap and refrigerated a few hours before steaming. The recipe amounts can easily be doubled.

WILD RICE PANCAKES

Serve these for breakfast with a maple or fruit syrup, or top with creamed chicken or turkey to make a substantial lunch or brunch dish.

3 large eggs, yolks separated
3/4 cup milk
2 tbs. melted unsalted butter
1/3 cup flour
3/4 tsp. kosher salt, or 1/2 tsp. regular salt
3/4 cup *Basic Cooked Wild Rice,* page 14
1/3 cup cooked crumbled bacon pieces

Preheat griddle. Separate eggs. Place egg yolks in a medium bowl and beat until well combined. Stir in milk, butter, flour and salt. Add wild rice. In a separate bowl, beat egg whites until stiff but not dry. Gently fold egg whites and bacon into rice mixture. Cook pancakes on lightly oiled griddle until set and lightly browned. Turn and cook on the second side. Serve immediately.

COMPANY BREAKFAST OATMEAL

Servings: 4

This is a great treat for a cold winter morning or when you want a tasty breakfast for the children.

1⅓ cups rolled oats (not quick cooking)
2 cups apple juice
¾ cup water
⅓ cup raisins
1 dash salt

Add ingredients to the rice cooker container. Stir and cover rice cooker. Turn on and cook oatmeal until rice cooker turns off. Stir once during cooking. After rice cooker shuts off, allow to stand for 10 minutes before serving.

WINE-POACHED PEARS

Riesling or other white wine makes a good poaching liquid for pears. For a dramatic pink blush, poach pears in red wine. Bosc, Anjou or Bartlett pears work well for poaching. The poaching liquid can be reduced a little and served with the chilled pears.

4 medium pears, firm but ripe
2 cups white wine
1/2 cup sugar
1/2 tsp. vanilla

Peel pears and remove core from bottom. Cut a slice from bottom of each pear to form a flat base. Leave stem on top of pear. Add wine and sugar to rice cooker container. Coat the cored pears with the wine mixture and lay them on their sides in the steamer tray. Place the steamer tray in the rice cooker, cover and cook the pears for about 20 minutes. Pears are cooked when the tip of a knife goes in easily. If the pears are still firm, continue to cook for another 3 to 5 minutes. Turn off cooker. Carefully remove steamer tray from cooker. When pears are cool enough to handle, move them to a bowl. Add vanilla to liquid and pour over pears. Chill for 1 to 2 hours or overnight in the refrigerator. Serve with whipped cream and toasted sliced almonds.

LEMON CUSTARD

Serve this lemony dessert with fresh berries or Steamed Rhubarb and Strawberries, *page 62.*

1 cup heavy cream
¼ cup sugar
1 dash salt

2 large eggs plus 2 egg yolks
½ tsp. vanilla extract
½ tsp. lemon extract

Combine cream and sugar; beat until sugar dissolves. Add remaining ingredients and mix well. Spray three 6-oz. custard cups with nonstick cooking spray. Pour custard mixture through a sieve into custard cups. Cover each cup with a small piece of aluminum foil, crimping foil around top of cup. Add about 3 cups water to rice cooker container. Place custard cups in steamer tray. Cover and allow to stand for about 20 minutes after water has come to a boil. Check one cup by carefully removing from rice cooker with tongs. If the mixture is not fairly firm to touch, re-cover cup with foil and return to rice cooker for 2 to 3 minutes additional steaming. Remove from rice cooker and allow to stand for a few minutes before serving, or chill for a few hours.

Note: You can also pour mixture into a 3-cup ovenproof dish that will fit into cooker. Cover with foil. After water comes to a boil, steam for 25 to 30 minutes.

STEAMED RHUBARB AND STRAWBERRIES

Strawberries and rhubarb are a classic combination. Steam them in the rice cooker and chill. Eat as a light dessert or serve on French toast or waffles for breakfast.

$1/2$ lb. rhubarb, trimmed and cut into 1-inch pieces
$1/2$ lb. strawberries, stemmed and quartered
$1/2$ cup sugar

Combine rhubarb, strawberries and sugar in a 7- to 8-inch stainless steel or deep glass dish with a 3-cup capacity that will fit in the steamer tray. Pour 2 cups water into the rice cooker container. Place dish with rhubarb and strawberries in steamer tray.

After water has come to a boil, steam fruit for 10 to 12 minutes. Carefully remove the lid and check to see if rhubarb is soft; if not, steam for another 2 to 3 minutes. When rhubarb is soft, carefully remove bowl from steamer tray and allow to cool.

For a free catalog of all Bristol Publishing books, call us toll-free at: 1-800-346-4889